Ethel Smith's Second PIANO and ORGAN Duet Album

Contents

ABIDE WITH ME	16
BLEST BE THE TIE THAT BINDS	20
DAY IS DYING IN THE WEST	28
FAITH OF OUR FATHERS	24
HE LEADETH ME	10
HOLY, HOLY, HOLY	6
I NEED THEE EVERY HOUR	32
JUST AS I AM	13
LEAD, KINDLY LIGHT	46
MY FAITH LOOKS UP TO THEE	41
MY JESUS, I LOVE THEE	35
NEARER, MY GOD, TO THEE	38
NOW THE DAY IS OVER	44
ROCK OF AGES	2

Copyright 1951
ETHEL SMITH MUSIC CORP.

ROCK OF AGES

Suggested Registration
For General Electronic or Pipe Organs
Upper: Flute 8', 4'
Piccolo 2'
Lower: Melodia 8'
Pedal: 16' Bourdon Soft
Tremolo - Small

Suggested Registration
For Pre-Set Organs
(A#) 00 5032 000
(A#) 00 4300 000
Pedal 4-3
Vibrato 2

Suggested Registration
For Spinet Drawbar Organs
(U) 00 5032 000
(L) 4300 0000
Pedal 3
Vibrato Small

THOMAS HASTINGS
Arr. by Ethel Smith

Copyright © 1951 by Ethel Smith Music Corp.
International Copyright Secured   Made in U.S.A.   All Rights Reserved

3

*Upper { Drawbars: 21 7645 111
          Other Organs: Add Trumpet 8'

**Lower { Drawbars: (00) 6845 322(0)
          Other Organs: Add Diapason 8'

5

HOLY, HOLY, HOLY

Suggested Registration
For General Electronic or Pipe Organs
Upper: Flutes 8', 4', Strings 8', Reeds 8'
Lower: Diapason 8', Strings 4'
Pedal: 16', 8' Medium
Tremolo - Small

Suggested Registration
For Pre-Set Organs
(A♯) 00 7856 430
(A♯) 00 5734 211
Pedal 5-3
Vibrato 1

Suggested Registration
For Spinet Drawbar Organs
(U) 00 7856 430
(L) 5734 2110
Pedal 4
Vibrato Small

Rev. JOHN B. DYKES
Arr. by Ethel Smith

Copyright ©1951 by Ethel Smith Music Corp.
International Copyright Secured   Made in U.S.A.   All Rights Reserved

7

8

9

HE LEADETH ME

Suggested Registration
For General Electronic or Pipe Organs
Upper: String Diapason 8'
Lower: Melodia 8'
Pedal: 16', 8' Soft
Tremolo - Small

Suggested Registration
For Pre-Set Organs
[A#] 00 4544 221
[A#] 00 3543 320
Pedal 4-3
Vibrato 1

Suggested Registration
For Spinet Drawbar Organs
[U] 00 4544 221
[L] 3543 3200
Pedal 3
Vibrato Small

WILLIAM B. BRADBURY
Arr. by Ethel Smith

Copyright ©1951 by Ethel Smith Music Corp.
International Copyright Secured   Made in U.S.A.   All Rights Reserved

Upper { Drawbars: 00 5200 000
Other Organs: Cancel Diap., Add Flute 8'

*Lower Drawbars: (00) 4200 000 (0)

* Upper { Increase to Full Swell   ** Lower { Increase to Full Great

JUST AS I AM

Suggested Registration
For General Electronic or Pipe Organs
Upper: Flutes 8', 4', Piccolo 2'
Lower: Melodia 8'
Pedal: 16', 8' Soft
Tremolo - Small

Suggested Registration
For Pre-Set Organs
[A#] 00 5032 000
[A#] 00 4300 000
Pedal 5-3
Vibrato 1

Suggested Registration
For Spinet Drawbar Organs
[U] 00 5032 000
[L] 4300 0000
Pedal 3
Vibrato Small

WILLIAM B. BRADBURY
Arr. by Ethel Smith

Copyright ©1951 by Ethel Smith Music Corp.
International Copyright Secured   Made in U.S.A.   All Rights Reserved

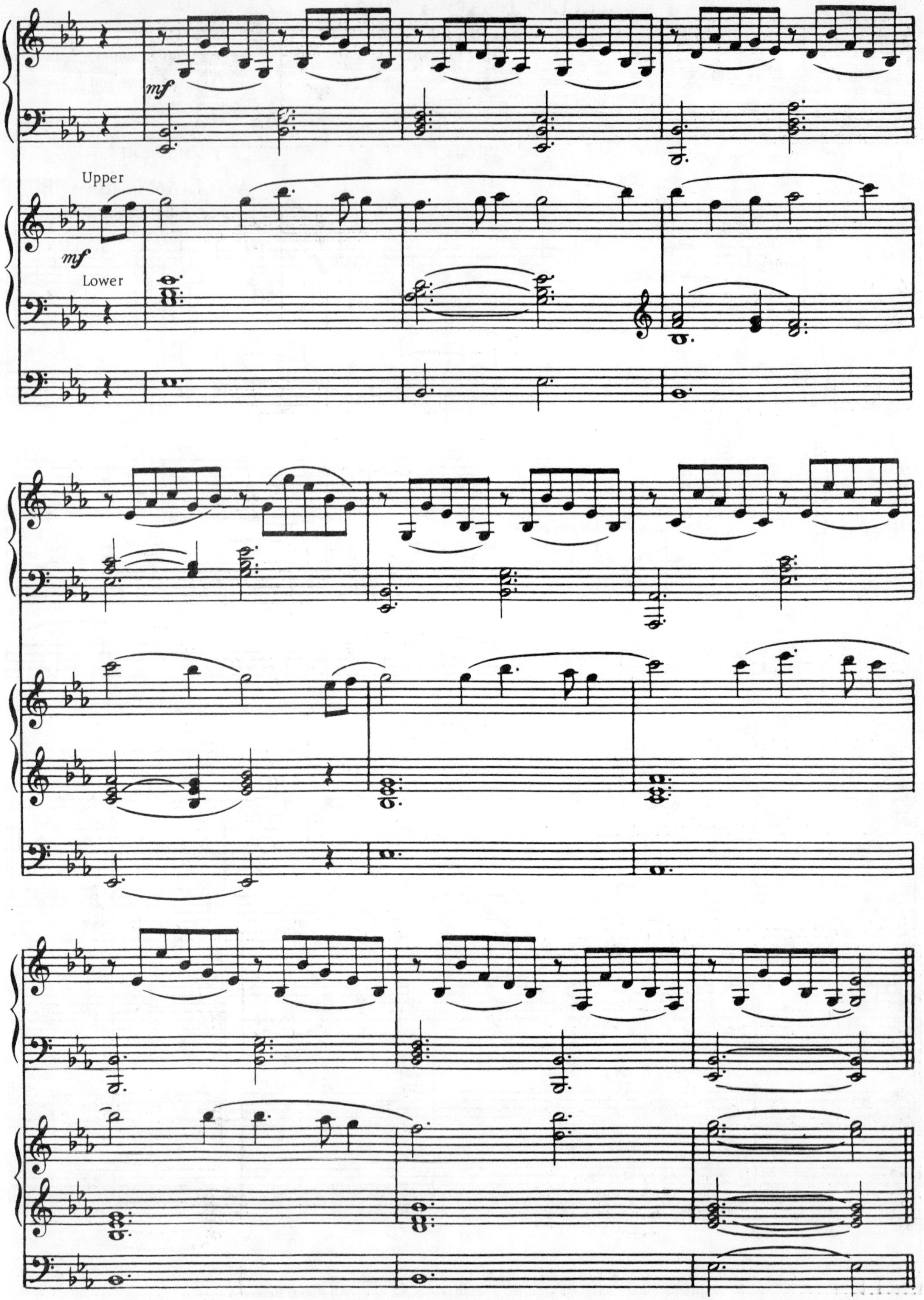
mf
Upper
mf
Lower

f
mf
Lower
mf
Upper
f
f
Upper
rit
Lower
Increase Lower Manual
rit

ABIDE WITH ME

Suggested Registration
For General Electronic or Pipe Organs
Upper: Stopped Diapason 8'
       Reed 4'
Lower: Melodia 8', Strings 4'
Pedal: 16', 8' Medium
Tremolo - Small

Suggested Registration
For Pre-Set Organs
[A#] 00 5533 210
[A#] 00 4533 110
Pedal 5-3
Vibrato 1

Suggested Registration
For Spinet Drawbar Organs
[U] 00 5533 210
[L] 4533 1100
Pedal 4
Vibrato Small

W. H. MONK
Arr. by Ethel Smith

Copyright ©1951 by Ethel Smith Music Corp.
International Copyright Secured   Made in U.S.A.   All Rights Reserved

Upper { Drawbars: 11 7644 111
{ Other Organs: Add Solo 8', Flute 8'

Lower { Drawbars: (00) 6844 321(0)
{ Other Organs: Add Diapason 8'

18

19

BLEST BE THE TIE THAT BINDS

Suggested Registration
For General Electronic or Pipe Organs
Upper: Oboe 8'
Lower: Melodia 8'
Pedal: 16' Bourdon
Tremolo - Small

Suggested Registration
For Pre-Set Organs
A♯ 00 3675 200
A♯ 00 4412 110
Pedal 5-3
Vibrato 2

Suggested Registration
For Spinet Drawbar Organs
U 00 3675 200
L 4412 1100
Pedal 4
Vibrato Small

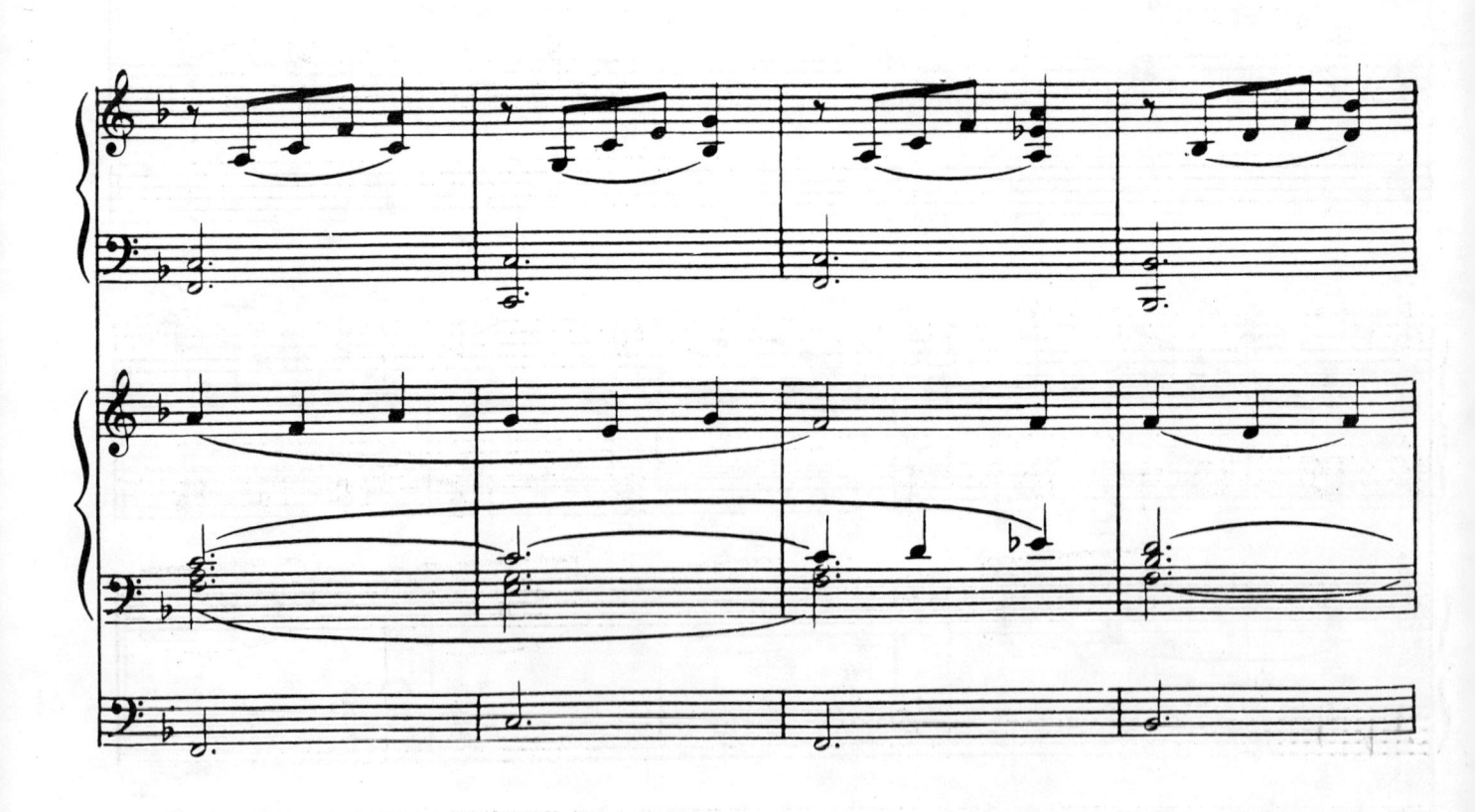

HANS G. NAEGELI
Arr. by Ethel Smith

Copyright ©1951 by Ethel Smith Music Corp.
International Copyright Secured   Made in U.S.A.   All Rights Reserved

21

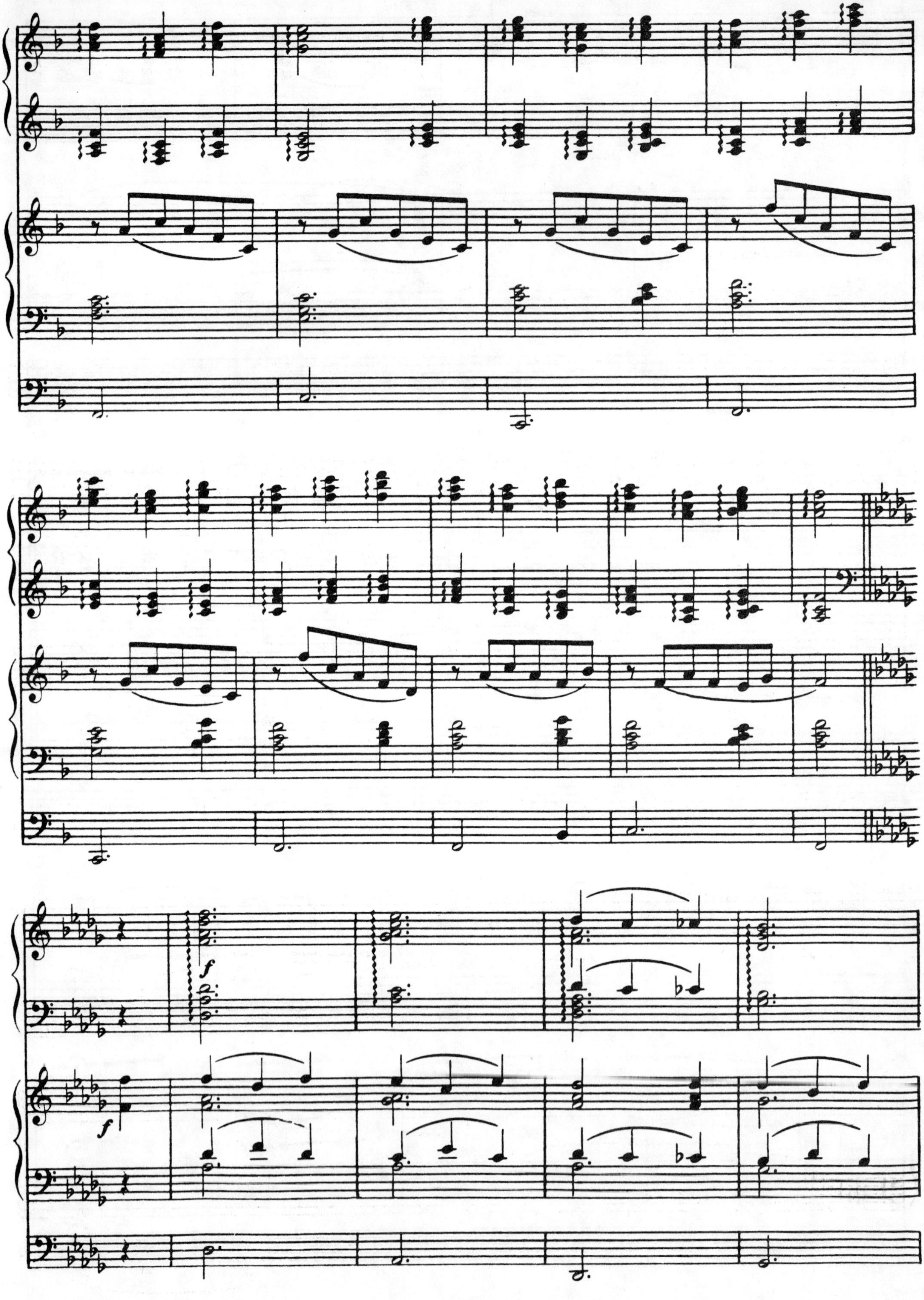
f
f

23

FAITH OF OUR FATHERS

Suggested Registration
For General Electronic or Pipe Organs
Upper: Flutes 8', 4', Reeds 4'
Lower: Melodia 8', Flute 4'
Pedal: 16', 8' Soft
Tremolo - Small

Suggested Registration
For Pre-Set Organs
A# 00 5534 210
A# 00 4434 110
Pedal 3-3
Vibrato 2

Suggested Registration
For Spinet Drawbar Organs
U 00 5534 210
L 4434 110
Pedal 3
Vibrato Small

H.F. HEMY
Arr. by Ethel Smith

Copyright ©1951 by Ethel Smith Music Corp.
International Copyright Secured   Made in U.S.A.   All Rights Reserved

25

26

27

DAY IS DYING IN THE WEST

Suggested Registration
For General Electronic or Pipe Organs
Upper: French Horn 8'
Lower: Melodia 8'
Pedal: 16', 8' Soft
Tremolo - Small

Suggested Registration
For Pre-Set Organs
[A#] 00 5310 000
[A#] 00 4512 110
Pedal 4-3
Vibrato 1

Suggested Registration
For Spinet Drawbar Organs
[U] 00 5310 000
[L] 4512 1100
Pedal 3
Vibrato Small

WILLIAM F. SHERWIN
Arr. by Ethel Smith

Copyright ©1951 by Ethel Smith Music Corp.
International Copyright Secured   Made in U.S.A.   All Rights Reserved

29

mp
mf
cresc.
mf
cresc.
Lower
f
Upper
Drawbars: 00 6876 540
Other Organs: Add trpt. 8'
f
Upper
Lower
Drawbars: (00) 6845 322(0)
Other Organs: Add Diapason 8'

31

I NEED THEE EVERY HOUR

Suggested Registration
For General Electronic or Pipe Organs
Upper: Flutes 8', 4', Oboe 8'
Strings 4'
Lower: Melodia 8', Flute 4',
French Horn 8'
Pedal: 16', 8' Medium
Tremolo - Small

Suggested Registration
For Pre-Set Organs
(A#) 00 4543 221
(A#) 00 6060 300
Pedal 4-3
Vibrato 1

Suggested Registration
For Spinet Drawbar Organs
(U) 00 4543 221
(L) 6060 3000
Pedal 3
Vibrato Small

REV. ROBERT LOWRY
Arr. by Ethel Smith

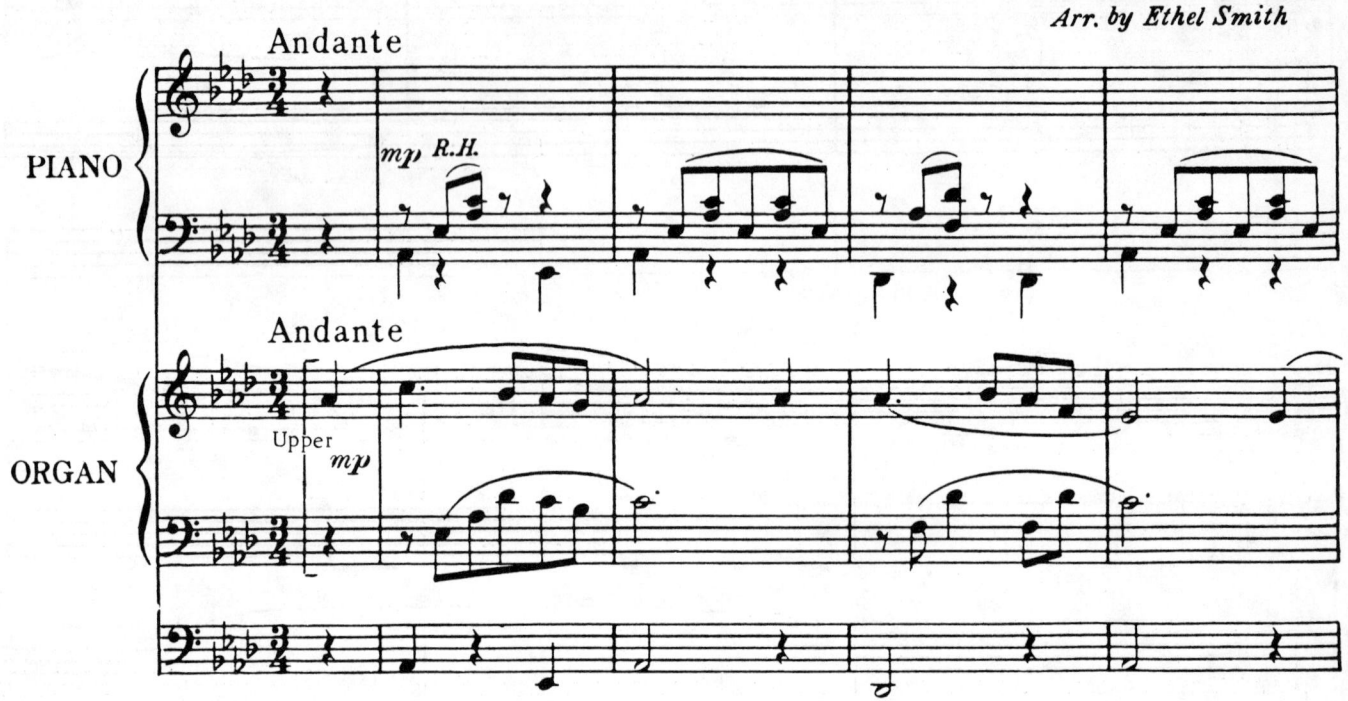

Copyright © 1951 by Ethel Smith Music Corp.
International Copyright Secured   Made in U.S.A.   All Rights Reserved

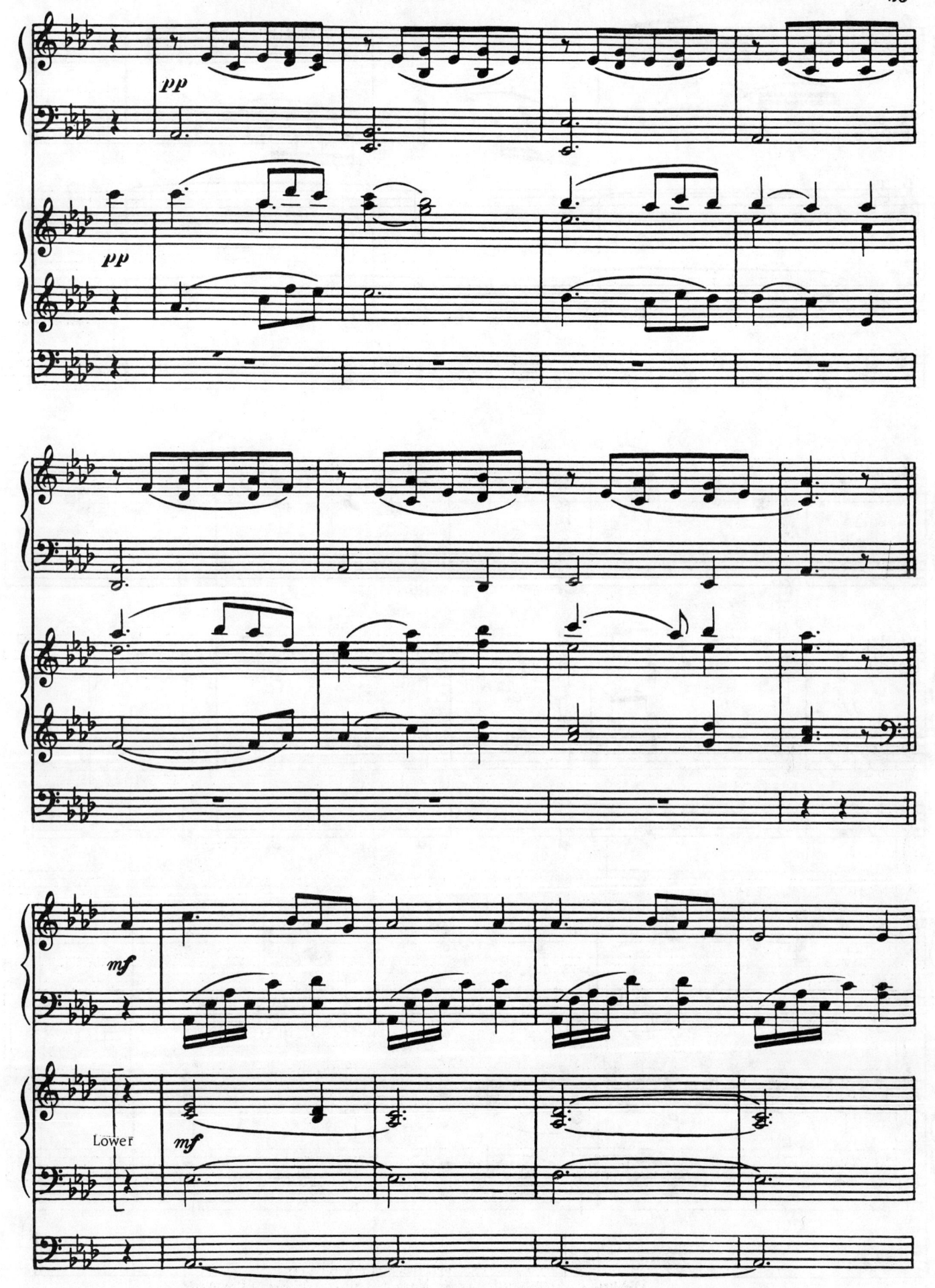
pp
pp
mf
Lower
mf

34

MY JESUS, I LOVE THEE

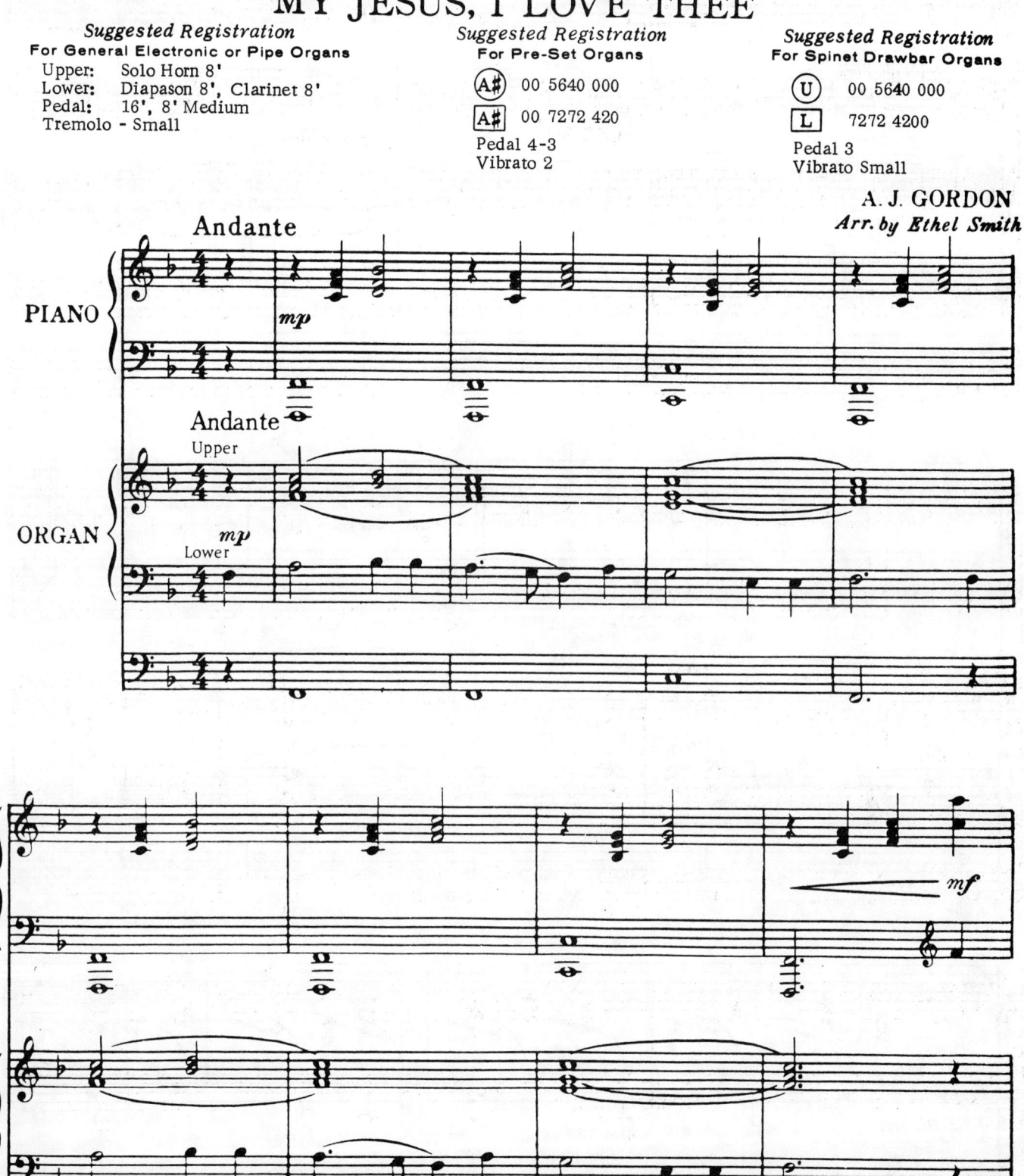

Suggested Registration
For General Electronic or Pipe Organs
Upper: Solo Horn 8'
Lower: Diapason 8', Clarinet 8'
Pedal: 16', 8' Medium
Tremolo - Small

Suggested Registration
For Pre-Set Organs
A♯ 00 5640 000
A♯ 00 7272 420
Pedal 4-3
Vibrato 2

Suggested Registration
For Spinet Drawbar Organs
U 00 5640 000
L 7272 4200
Pedal 3
Vibrato Small

A. J. GORDON
Arr. by Ethel Smith

Copyright © 1951 by Ethel Smith Music Corp.
International Copyright Secured   Made in U.S.A.   All Rights Reserved

* Drawbars: (00) 5734 210(0)
Other Organs: Cancel Clarinet 8'

37

NEARER, MY GOD, TO THEE

Suggested Registration
For General Electronic or Pipe Organs
Upper: Strings 4'
Lower: Melodia 8', Strings 8'
Pedal: 16' Bourdon
Tremolo - Small

Suggested Registration
For Pre-Set Organs
A# 00 1221 011
A# 00 4434 100
Pedal 6-3
Vibrato 2

Suggested Registration
For Spinet Drawbar Organs
U 00 1221 011
L 4434 1000
Pedal 5
Vibrato Small

LOWELL MASON
Arr. by Ethel Smith

Copyright ©1951 by Ethel Smith Music Corp.
International Copyright Secured   Made in U.S.A.   All Rights Reserved

39

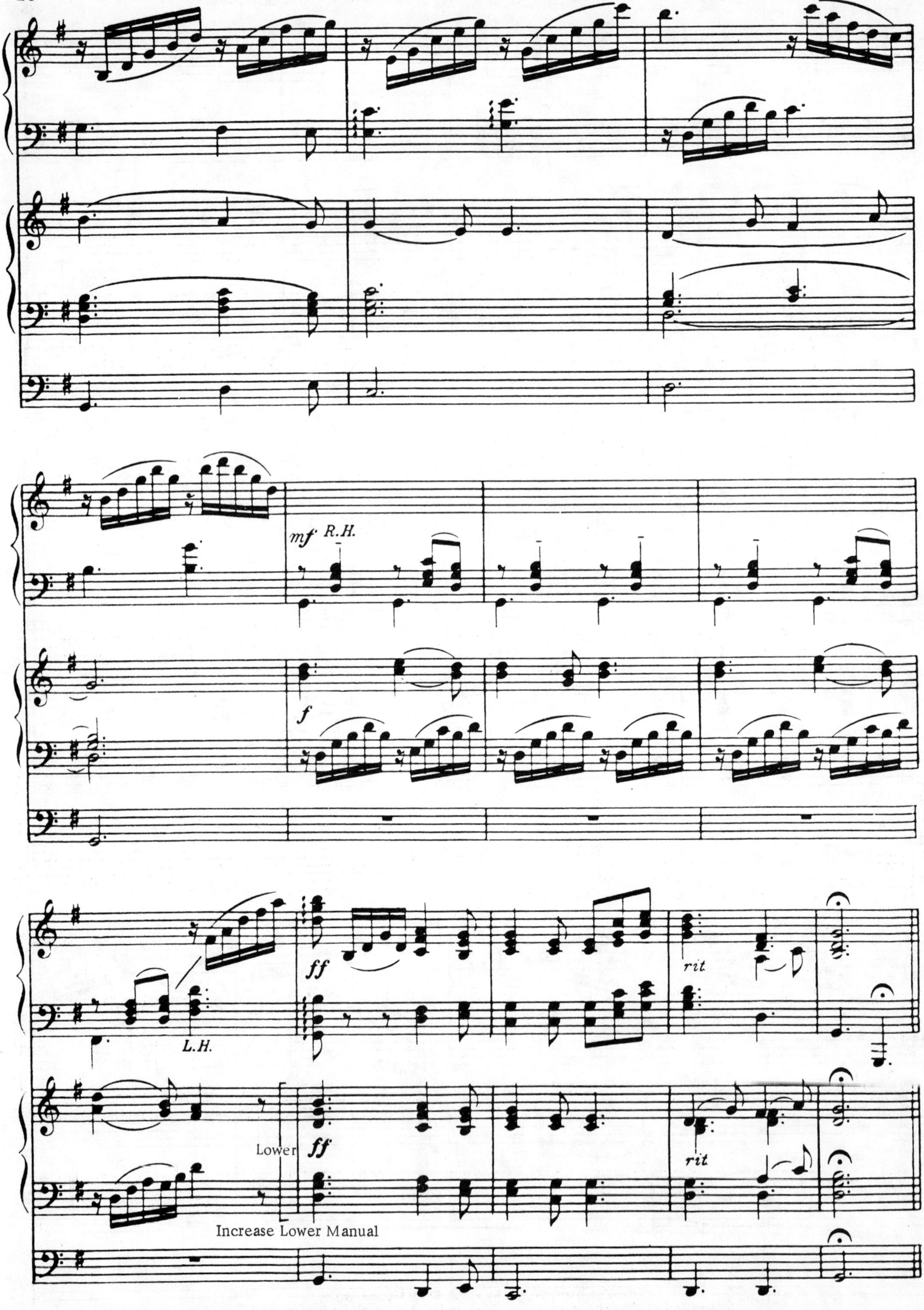
mf R.H.
f
L.H.
ff
rit
Lower
ff
rit
Increase Lower Manual

MY FAITH LOOKS UP TO THEE

Suggested Registration
For General Electronic or Pipe Organs
Upper: Stopped Diapason 8'
Lower: Diapason 8', Strings 4'
Pedal: 16', 8' Soft
Tremolo - Small

Suggested Registration
For Pre-Set Organs

A♯   00 4411 110
A♯   00 6853 321
Pedal 4-3
Vibrato 1

Suggested Registration
For Spinet Drawbar Organs

U   00 4411 110
L   6853 3210
Pedal 3
Vibrato Small

LOWELL MASON
Arr. by Ethel Smith

Copyright ©1951 by Ethel Smith Music Corp.
International Copyright Secured   Made in U.S.A.   All Rights Reserved

41

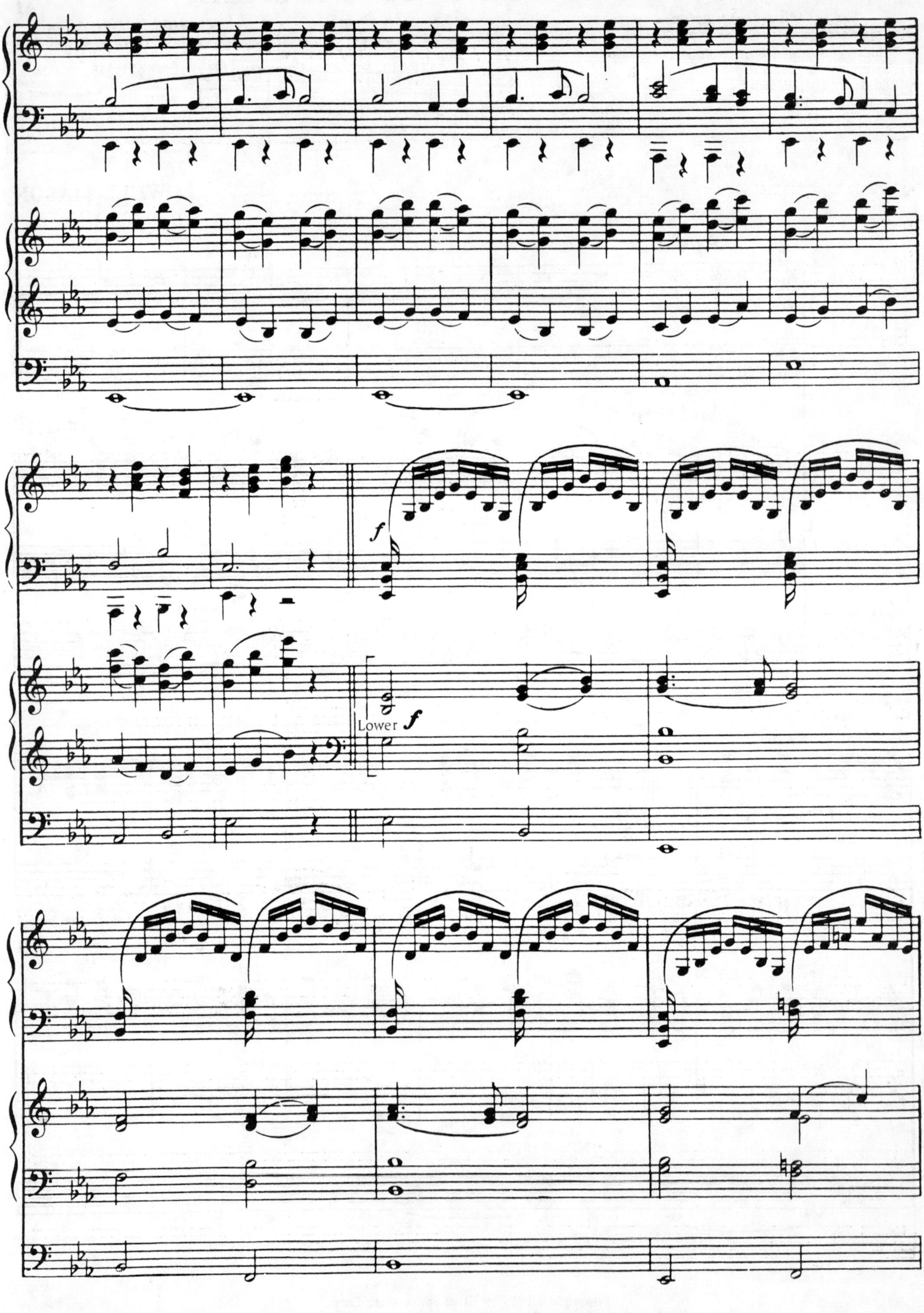
f
Lower f

43

NOW THE DAY IS OVER

Suggested Registration
For General Electronic or Pipe Organs
Upper: Oboe 8'
Lower: Melodia 8', Strings 8', 4'
Pedal: 16', 8' Medium
Tremolo - Small

Suggested Registration
For Pre-Set Organs
[A#] 00 3675 200
[A#] 00 6634 211
Pedal 4-3
Vibrato 2

Suggested Registration
For Spinet Drawbar Organs
[U] 00 3675 200
[L] 6634 2110
Pedal 3
Vibrato Small

JOSEPH BARNBY
Arr. by Ethel Smith

Copyright ©1951 by Ethel Smith Music Corp.
International Copyright Secured   Made in U.S.A.   All Rights Reserved

45

LEAD, KINDLY LIGHT

Suggested Registration
For General Electronic or Pipe Organs
Upper: Oboe 8'
Lower: Diapason 8', Flute 4'
Pedal: 16', 8' Medium
Tremolo - Small

Suggested Registration
For Pre-Set Organs
A♯ 00 3665 200
A♯ 00 6262 320
Pedal 5-3
Vibrato 1

Suggested Registration
For Spinet Drawbar Organs
U 00 3665 200
L 6262 3200
Pedal 4
Vibrato Small
(Vibrato Chorus Optional)

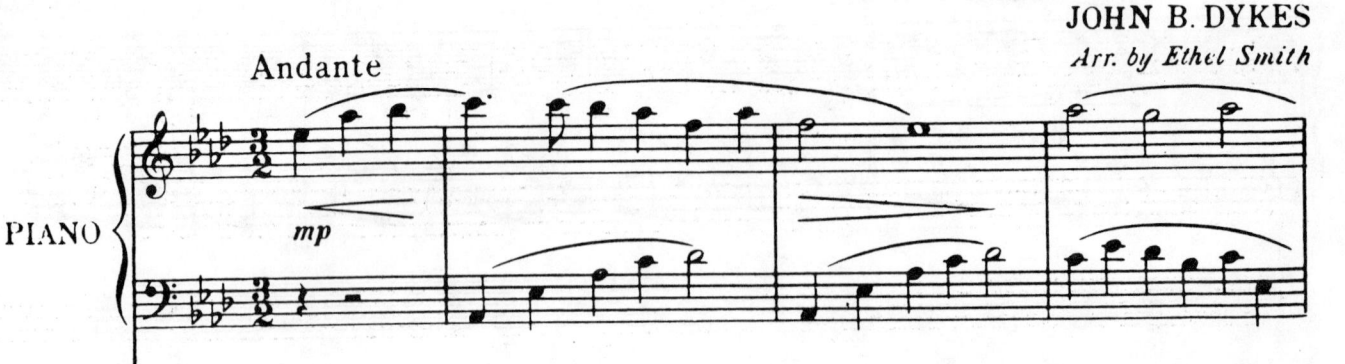

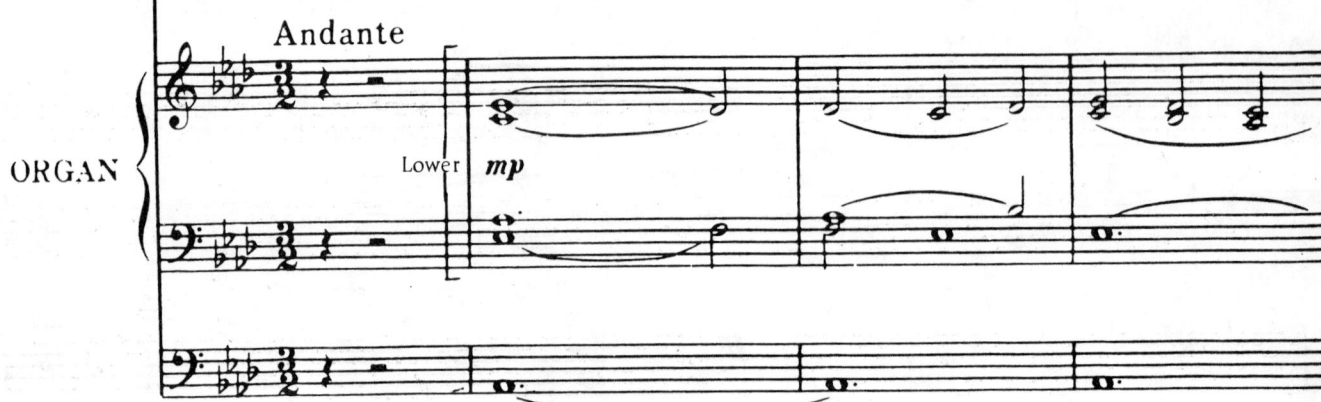

JOHN B. DYKES
Arr. by Ethel Smith

Copyright © 1951 by Ethel Smith Music Corp.
International Copyright Secured   Made in U.S.A.   All Rights Reserved

47

48